PHENOMENAL F.A. CUP

PHENOMENAL F.A.CUP

MICHAEL COLEMAN

www.michael-coleman.com

Illustrated by
Mike Phillips

Hippo

For all the staff at Fareham Library –
where would I be without you?

Scholastic Children's Books,
Commonwealth House, 1–19 New Oxford Street,
London WC1A 1NU, UK
A division of Scholastic Ltd
London ~ New York ~ Toronto ~ Sydney ~ Auckland
Mexico City ~ New Delhi ~ Hong Kong

Published in the UK by Scholastic Ltd, 2001

ISBN 0 439 99498 5

Typeset by TW Typesetting, Midsomer Norton, Somerset
Printed and bound by Bath Press, Bath

2 4 6 8 10 9 7 5 3 1

Contents

INTRODUCTION

Football can be foul – especially when your team keeps on losing! But in the phenomenal FA Cup even the worst teams have a chance of glory…

The FA Cup (or the FA Challenge Cup to give it its full name) has grown phenomenally. Starting with just 15 teams, the competition is now entered by well over 600. Some of the teams are fantastic – but plenty are pretty feeble. That's what has made the FA Cup so phenomenally successful.

In what other competition but the FA Cup could minuscule Mangotsfield United be just one place behind mighty Manchester United and awful Argonauts FC a long way ahead of awesome Arsenal?

(You want to know how? Easy – alphabetically, Mangotsfield were immediately behind Manchester United in the list of entries for the 1998–99 FA Cup ... and Argonauts FC entered the FA Cup for the one and only time in 1879, ten years before Arsenal had even played a match.)

The competition has produced a whole host of phenomenal matches between phenomenal teams of phenomenal players – and you'll be reading about plenty of them in this book. Like...

- the **phenomenal** match which lasted for 11 hours!
- the **phenomenal** team who couldn't afford their train fares!
- the **phenomenal** player who nearly lost his head!

Most of all though, the phenomenal FA Cup is famous for the way it gives little teams the chance to pit themselves against the giants of the game. When that happens, the big teams go frantic with worry – and in this book you'll find out why! You'll read some frantic facts that the top teams of today would prefer not to remember. Like the times when...

- a frantic Arsenal were beaten by a team which cost less than their own players' boots
- a frantic Manchester United came up against a joke team and found it wasn't at all funny
- a frantic Aston Villa lost their hold on the FA Cup without even getting changed

And, as always, we'll confer our very own phenomenal *Foul Football* awards on the powerful personalities who have played their part in making the FA Cup the world-famous competition it is today. Awards like...

 THE MOST PHENOMENALLY STUPID EVEN THOUGH IT WAS TRUE FA CUP QUOTE AWARD...

Terry McDermott, winner with Liverpool and losing assistant manager with Newcastle United, who explained how difficult it is to win the competition in the immortal words...

NO ONE HANDS YOU CUPS ON A PLATE, Y'KNOW!

So don't just sit there, read on! FA Cup football is phenomenal!

THE PHENOMENAL FA CUP TIMELINE

1863 The "FA" part of the FA Cup comes into being. A man named Ebenezer Cobb Morley (not to be confused with Ebenezer Scrooge) calls a meeting of 12 football clubs in and around London. They band together and call themselves the Football Association (FA).

1871 (20 July) The FA's next secretary, Charles William Alcock, makes a proposal:

They talked like that in 1871. What Alcock meant was: "How about having a competition and calling it the FA Cup?"

1871 (November) They may have talked slowly in those days but they moved fast. Four months later 15 teams have entered and the first FA Cup ties are played.

1872 A team called the Wanderers win the first FA Cup Final in front of a crowd of 2,000.

1873 The Wanderers reach their second final – without playing a game! As reigning Cup-holders they go straight into the final with all the other teams playing for the right to "challenge" them. The Wanderers are even allowed to choose the ground! Not surprisingly, they win the Cup again.

1874 The challenging idea is scrapped – and, for once, the Wanderers find the competition too challenging (though they bounce back to win it three times in a row between 1876–8). The Cup

is won by the Royal Engineers. They're another Southern team of ex-public schoolboys – just like the winners each year after until...

1883 At last! For the first time the Cup is won by a team from the north of England, Blackburn Olympic. What's more, the players who beat Old Etonians are all working men. They include three weavers, a cotton worker, an iron worker, a picture framer, a plumber ... and a dentist's assistant named T. Hacking!

1887 Preston North End beat Hyde 26-0 (still the record FA Cup win). The Preston players ask for the Hyde goalkeeper's autograph because he plays so well!

THE PHENOMENALLY COURAGEOUS "CARRY ON AFTER GETTING A RECORD THUMPING" AWARD...

Hyde FC. Yes, the team Preston gave a good hyde-ing to didn't go into hiding – they're still playing today (though in 1919 they changed their name to Hyde United FC).

1888 About 150 teams enter for the 1888–89 competition. To stop one-sided games (like 26-0) some rubbish teams have to play "qualifying" matches before they get into the first "proper" round.

1915 World War One has started, but the competition hasn't stopped. Critics say it's all wrong, footballers should be pulverizing the enemy instead of each other. The FA Cup ceases until 1919.

1923 After being played on various grounds over the years, the Cup Final moves to the brand-new Wembley stadium. Well over 200,000 spectators get in. The stadium's only built for 125,000 so about half of them end up on the

touchlines. From now on Cup Finals will be all-ticket instead of pay-at-the-gate (or, in this case, climb-over-the-gate).

1925 After various changes the competition ends up the way it is today, with the big noises of the top two divisions not having to get their boots on until the third round.

1927 Fans who can't get tickets no longer have to wait for the Sunday papers to find out who won. The FA Cup Final is broadcast on the radio for the first time.

1935 Now they don't have to wait to see who their team will be playing, either. The draw for the third round is broadcast live. As it's on radio, the BBC producer in charge asks Stanley Rous, the FA Secretary making the draw, to give the bag of balls a good loud shake!

1938 The whole of the Cup Final is shown on a new-fangled invention called TV for the first time. It's watched by a massive audience of … 10,000!

1940 No messing about this time. When World War Two starts in September 1939, football stops at once. Critics say it's all wrong, the players should be playing because football matches raise the spectator's spirits! War Cup competitions begin, but the real FA Cup isn't played for again until…

1945 For the first and only time, matches before the semi-finals are played as home and away ties over two legs, without replays. If the teams are level at the end of the second game they keep going until somebody scores. (The FA Cup competition has invented the "golden goal" tie-breaker 50 years before the World Cup!)

1990 FA Cup draws are televised, with footballers that nobody of school age has ever seen play drawing the balls from a plastic goldfish bowl with all the water and goldfish removed (which is a pity, because they would liven the whole thing up a bit).

1994 The competition gets a sponsor. Instead of the majestically simple "FA Cup" it's now supposed to be called "The FA Cup sponsored by Littlewoods Pools". Critics are told to be grateful. If an offer in 1988 from Australian lager makers had been accepted its name would have been changed to "The Fosters Cup".

1998 The FA Cup gets a new sponsor, the insurance company AXA. Critics say it's not right, they're not English. And for once they *are* right. AXA are a French company. The Cup is still called the FA Cup, though. Just as well – the FA Tasse wouldn't sound right!

IT'S A KNOCKOUT!

The FA Cup is a knockout competition. A draw is held to decide which team should play which. The losers of each game (or "Cup-tie") are "knocked-out", while the winners go into the next round to play one of the other winners. This goes on until only one team is left ... at which point they've won the Cup!

But what happens if an FA Cup match ends in a draw (in other words, if a Cup-tie ends in a tie)?

- In 1872, the first year of the competition, *both* teams carried on to the next round! This all got very confusing, so...

- Replays were introduced. If a replay was a draw (even after 30 minutes of extra time) there was another replay – and so on until there was a winner. The same went for the Cup Final.

- This was fine while Cup Finals were usually being decided on Cup Final day. But after the finals in 1910, 1911 and 1912 all went to replays, extra time was brought in for the Cup Final.

- Replays could lead to some long matches. The record was set in 1971, when Alvechurch finally beat Oxford City 1-0 in the fourth qualifying round ... after six matches. Including extra time,

17

that's a gruelling 11 hours! The winners were promptly beaten in the next round – probably because they were still dead beat!

- Marathon replays ended in 1991, being replaced by penalty shoot-outs at the end of a single drawn replay. Was this because modern-day footballers lack the stamina? No, it was because police forces insisted on at least ten days notice between a Cup-tie and a replay.

WE NEED TEN DAYS TO SORT OUT WHO WANTS TO GO TO THE GAME!

Round numbers

The FA Cup ends at Wembley with the Cup Final in May. But when does it start?

- January?
- October?
- August?

Answer: August. That's when the 500 or so non-league teams who enter the competition every year start to play their qualifying rounds, hoping to be one of the 32 who go on to the competition "proper" and join the league clubs. By then they'll already have played five Cup-ties ... and will still be seven wins away from the Final! This is how it goes from the first round onwards.

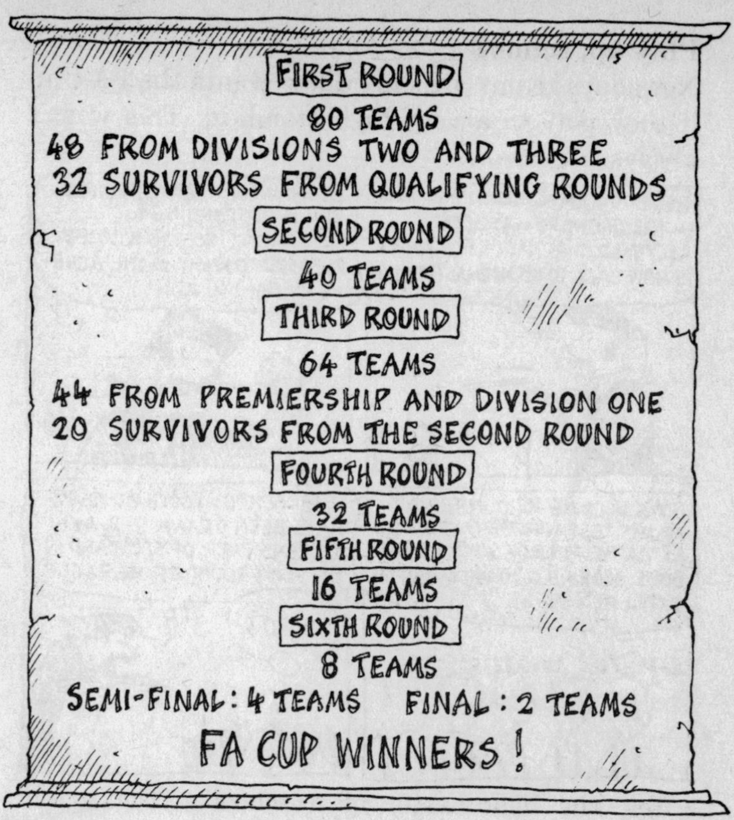

FIRST ROUND

80 TEAMS
48 FROM DIVISIONS TWO AND THREE
32 SURVIVORS FROM QUALIFYING ROUNDS

SECOND ROUND

40 TEAMS

THIRD ROUND

64 TEAMS
44 FROM PREMIERSHIP AND DIVISION ONE
20 SURVIVORS FROM THE SECOND ROUND

FOURTH ROUND

32 TEAMS

FIFTH ROUND

16 TEAMS

SIXTH ROUND

8 TEAMS

SEMI-FINAL: 4 TEAMS   FINAL: 2 TEAMS

FA CUP WINNERS!

THE MOST PHENOMENALLY PERSISTENT NO-HOPERS AWARD...

Marlow (of the Ryman league), the only team to have played in every single FA Cup tournament. They were beaten semi-finalists (as Great Marlow) in 1881–82, but since the start of the 20th century their best run was to the third round in 1992–3, when Tottenham Hotspur beat them 5-1.

Play up, school!

Nowadays teams are only allowed into the FA Cup if they play to a very high standard. This wasn't always the case...

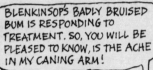

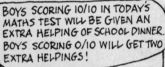

Yes, the headmaster of a school – Donington Grammar School in Lincolnshire – really did enter his team for the first-ever FA Cup competition in 1872. He thought his boys needed good healthy exercise and this was one of his enterprising schemes for giving it to them (another was to bring in an army sergeant to run their PE sessions!).

He reckoned without the luck of the draw, though. Donington were drawn away to the powerful Scottish team, Queens Park. The school couldn't afford the fares to Scotland, so had to drop out. They never entered again.

There were some Scots teams, some Irish teams and some Welsh teams...

...and they all took part in the FA Cup in the early years. Wrexham, the oldest team in Wales, first took part in 1883. Three Irish teams have played in the FA Cup: Cliftonville, Linfield Athletic and Distillery, a team formed by Belfast whiskey-producers.

Only one of these existing Scottish league teams has *not* taken part in the FA Cup. Which one?

CELTIC · RANGERS · HEARTS · QUEENS PARK · PARTICK THISTLE · THIRD LANARK

Answer: Celtic. All kicked out the Cup-holders Renton (who actually 1887), played between 1872 and 1888. Queen Olympik were twice runners-up and Blackburn Olympik were twice runners-up and ...ners, plus Cowlairs and Rangers once b... en semi-finalists.

But then, in 1888, the Scottish and Irish teams were knocked out for good. By a powerful team? No, by their own Football Associations! Both the Scottish and Irish FA Cup competitions had started (in 1873–74 and 1880–81 respectively) and the two FA's wanted to make sure their top teams took part in their own competition, not the foreign "English" FA Cup!

The Welsh FA aren't such spoilsports. They've always allowed their teams to enter the Welsh Cup and the FA Cup. (See "Phenomenal FA Cup Finals: 1927" for the time when Arsenal wished they hadn't!)

Frantic First

The FA Cup was the first football knockout competition, and has been clocking up firsts ever since. See if you can match these "firsts" with the year in which they took place.

Year	The first time...
1890	Ⓐ a period of extra time was played in a Cup Final.
1894	Ⓑ the Cup Final was played in May.
1913	Ⓒ the FA Cup third round was played in March.
1920	Ⓓ a player scored a Cup Final hat-trick.
1930	Ⓔ a team was officially awarded third place in the FA Cup.
1937	Ⓕ someone missed a penalty in a Cup Final.
1963	Ⓖ a player was sent off in a Cup Final.
1970	Ⓗ Cup Final teams had their names and squad numbers on their shirts.
1972	Ⓘ an FA Cup game was decided by a penalty shoot-out.
1985	Ⓙ a team from the Second Division won the FA Cup.
1993	Ⓚ the two Cup Final teams came out side-by-side.

Answers:

1890 – D William Townley of Blackburn Rovers in their 6-1 defeat of The Wednesday (now Sheffield Wednesday).

LOOKS LIKE WEDNESDAY DON'T KNOW WHAT DAY IT IS!

1894 – J Notts County, who beat Bolton Wanderers just one year after the Second Division was formed.

1913 – F Charlie Wallace (Aston Villa) – though it didn't matter; Villa still beat Sunderland 1-0.

1920 – A The rule had been introduced in 1913, after three finals in a row had needed replays. Until then extra time had been allowed in replays, but not in the Cup Final itself.

1930 – K The teams were Huddersfield Town and Arsenal, who came out together because Arsenal's manager, Herbert Chapman, had previously been the manager of Huddersfield.

1937 – B It then went back to its usual spot in April until 1952. Since then it's always taken place in May. (The first 11 finals were played in March!)

1963 – C Terrible snow and frost caused so many postponements that the 64 third round games due to be played on 5 January, weren't completed until 11 March.

1970 – E Not many people know this! Between 1970–74, third place matches were held between the beaten FA Cup semi-finalists. They were awful, mainly because beaten semi-finalists generally want to forget they *are* beaten semi-finalists and not prolong the agony. After just five years the idea was scrapped.

1972 – I Even though they weren't properly introduced until 1991? Yes. The third-place match between Birmingham City and Stoke City was decided on penalties after ending 0-0.

1985 – G Kevin Moran of Manchester United (who still beat Everton 1-0). As extra punishment, Moran wasn't allowed to go up and collect his medal. He had to wait for it to be posted to him, seven weeks later.

1993 – H Arsenal and Sheffield Wednesday – although Leicester City had had their names on their tracksuit tops for their 1961 Cup Final against Tottenham Hotspur. The Spurs captain, Danny Blanchflower, wasn't impressed. When the royal guest, the Duchess of Kent, asked why his team hadn't done the same he told her, "We know each other, Ma'am!"

THE FIRST-EVER CUP-WINNERS' PHENOMENALLY SILLY CELEBRATION AWARD...

Lord Arthur Kinnaird (The Wanderers and Old Etonians) who, in 1882, celebrated his fifth Cup-winner's medal by standing on his head in front of the grandstand.

25

Lifting The Trophy

Schoolboys (and schoolgirls) dream of lifting the FA Cup aloft. But, in 1895, one mystery man did more than dream of lifting it...

Yes, on the night of Wednesday 12 September 1895, a bold burglar "lifted" the FA Cup – and it was never seen again!

Aston Villa had won the Cup that April and one of their directors, William McGregor, had loaned the trophy to a boot and shoe shop to display in their window. In the middle of the night the thief cut a hole in the roof, dropped into the window and snaffled the cup. Then, leaving behind all the boots and shoes, he left the scene hot-foot!

The thief (or gang of thieves – nobody knows) was never found. Neither was the cup. A reward was offered for its safe return, but by then it had almost certainly been melted down to make counterfeit coins.

Aston Villa, the Cup-winners turned Cup-losers, were fined by the FA. How much?

- £25
- £250
- £2,500

Answer: £25 – because that's how much it cost to have a replacement made!

THE MOST PHENOMENALLY ACCURATE FORTUNE-TELLING FOOTBALLER AWARD...

Sam Warburton, captain of Blackburn Olympic, who'd said after his team won the FA Cup in 1883:

IT'LL NEVER GO BACK TO LONDON!

He was right. Northern and Midlands clubs won the Cup every year until the Aston Villa burglary – and then it never went anywhere again.

Trophy teasers

1 The original FA Cup trophy was 46 cm high, had two handles, and a model of a footballer on the top. (Just in case you find it in your back garden one day!) It cost £20 to make and was nicknamed ... what?

a) Little silver idol.

b) Little tin idol.

c) Little gold idol.

2 Apart from costing £5 more, trophy number two was identical to the first. It lasted until 1910, when it was given away. Why?

a) One of the handles had fallen off.

b) The cup's design had been copied and dozens of replicas existed.

c) Somebody discovered it wasn't made of silver.

3 The design of FA Cup number three (the same design as today's cup) was registered so that it couldn't be copied. The new cup cost £52.50, and was made by a company in Bradford. Who, in 1911, were its first winners?

a) Bradford City.

b) Blackburn Olympic.

c) Aston Villa.

4 FA Cup number four was put into use in 1992 and is still in use today. It's identical in every way to cup number three which, although pretty worn out after

80 years of being thrown in the air by Cup-winning teams, is still brought out for appearances at special events like televised Cup draws. The first winners of the new trophy were Liverpool. What did they do with the new trophy before taking it on a triumphant tour of the city?

a) Wrap it in cotton wool.

b) Tie the wrong colour ribbons to it.

c) Damage it.

5 FA Cup number five was made in 1993. Why?

a) In case the Bradford Burglar was still in business.

b) In case Liverpool ever won it again.

c) Just in case.

Answers: 1b) Even though it was made of silver! **2b)** They were being played for in local cup competitions and the FA thought that the winners of their competition should receive a different trophy to the winners of the Clogwell and District Cup. Lord Kinnaird had just completed 21 years as FA President, so FA Cup number two was awarded to him as a present. **3a)** It's the only time they've ever won it! **4c)** After which the brand new lid no longer fitted on the brand new cup! The club had to have it fixed before they gave it back. **5 All three, but mostly c)** It's locked away in a bank in case of emergencies ... and cost exactly £12,403.30.

THAT WILL BE £12,400 FOR THE CUP AND £3.30 FOR MY BUS FARE, PLEASE

FOOTBALL ASSOCIATION

The F(lattening) A(ttempt) Cup

But for a stroke of phenomenally good fortune another trophy would have had to be made. Portsmouth, who'd won the 1939 FA Cup Final, suddenly found themselves Cup-holders for the next six years! World War Two had begun and although special war-time cup competitions were played, the FA Cup itself was abandoned until the war ended in 1945.

However, not only was Portsmouth the home of the Cup-holders, it was also the home of most of the warships of the Royal Navy. If any football club was going to have a bomb land on its trophy room it was Portsmouth FC! So the club decided to put the FA Cup into the vaults of a local bank for safe keeping.

They'd take it out to show off on match days and to be given the occasional polish by the Portsmouth FC tea lady, but afterwards it was always straight back to the bank.

Then, one night, over came the bombers. Boom! Portsmouth took a pounding. Fratton Park, Portsmouth's ground didn't get hit, even though it was right next door to an important railway yard. But elsewhere in the city bombs landed on streets, houses, shops … and banks. With one bomb flattening one bank in particular!

So it was a great relief to all concerned when into Fratton Park the next morning strolled manager Jack Tinn with an undamaged FA Cup under his arm. Luckily, he'd taken it out of the bank on the morning of the air raid – and then spent the whole night at home cuddling it while he was crouched in a cupboard beneath the stairs!

PHENOMENAL FA CUP FINALS: 1901 SHEFFIELD UNITED V. TOTTENHAM HOTSPUR

By the start of the 1900–01 season the Football League had grown to two divisions. There were the 18 fancy fliers of the First Division (such as Bury and Notts County) and a further 18 solid scrappers in the Second Division. Of these 36 teams, just one was based in the south of England – a team called Woolwich Arsenal (later simply Arsenal, but always nicknamed "The Gunners") who were in with the solid scrappers.

Tottenham Hotspur and the other top teams in London and the south of England played in the soft (according to northerners!) Southern League, only being allowed out to meet Football League teams in the FA Cup.

So, how many soft southerners did Tottenham (then, as now, nicknamed "Spurs") have in their team?

Answer: None! They had five Scots, two Welsh-men, one Irishman – and three English players, all of whom came from the Midlands and the north. And they were brainy! They had to be...

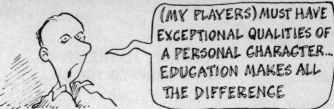

TOTTENHAM'S PLAYER-MANAGER, JOHN CAMERON

(MY PLAYERS) MUST HAVE EXCEPTIONAL QUALITIES OF A PERSONAL CHARACTER... EDUCATION MAKES ALL THE DIFFERENCE

One of his players was a Scottish goal-machine named Sandy Brown. Fancy yourself as a goal-getter? This was Brown's phenomenal FA Cup goalscoring record:

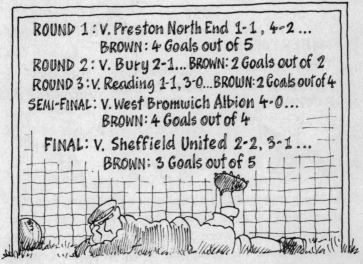

ROUND 1 : V. Preston North End 1-1 , 4-2 ...
BROWN : 4 Goals out of 5
ROUND 2 : V. Bury 2-1... BROWN: 2 Goals out of 2
ROUND 3 : V. Reading 1-1, 3-0...BROWN: 2 Goals out of 4
SEMI-FINAL : V. West Bromwich Albion 4-0...
BROWN: 4 Goals out of 4
FINAL : V. Sheffield United 2-2, 3-1 ...
BROWN: 3 Goals out of 5

Sandy Brown's 15 goals (out of 20) set two FA Cup records. He was the first player to score in every round, and his total in a single Cup run is still the highest ever scored.

Spurs and Sheffield drew 2-2 in their first phenomenal final, thanks to a famously frantic goal. With Spurs 2-1 ahead...

A SHEFFIELD SHOOTER SHOT...

CLAWLEY IN THE SPURS GOAL DROPPED THE BALL...

ONLY FOR CLAWLEY TO CLAW IT BACK...

AND PUSH IT ROUND THE POST...

WHEREUPON THE LINESMAN FLAGGED FOR A CORNER...

CLAWLEY WENT TO TAKE A GOAL KICK...

THE REF AWARDED A GOAL!

So the game went to a replay, which Spurs won 2-1 after being a goal down. They are the only non-league (as they were then) club ever to win the FA Cup since the inception of the Football League in 1888–89, and their famous victory led to wild celebrations.

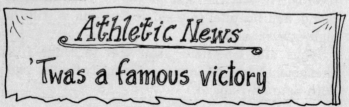

Athletic News

'Twas a famous victory

34

In the middle of these celebrations, somebody did something to the FA Cup itself that had never been done before. Did they...

a) use it as a portable loo?

b) fill it with jellied eels and other London delicacies?

c) tie ribbons to it in Spurs' colours?

Answer: c) They began the tradition of tying ribbons to it. (And you thought the cup's handles were for carrying it around, eh?)

THE FA CUP-HOLDERS PHENOMENALLY PATHETIC PERFORMANCE THE FOLLOWING SEASON AWARD...

Tottenham Hotspur. The following season they were knocked out in the first round – by Southampton, a fellow Southern League side!

HOW EMBARRASSING!

35

COLOSSAL CROWDS AND GRACIOUS GROUNDS

The first FA Cup Final in 1872 was watched by just 2,000 fans. But as the popularity of the competition grew, so did the crowds. Sometimes their behaviour has been phenomenally fair and sometimes it's been frantically foul…

What a ropey match!

In 1913 it couldn't have been fairer. A massive 120,081 fans packed in to watch the final between Aston Villa and Sunderland. How were they separated from the pitch? By just a piece of rope!

I'LL BE GLAD WHEN I GROW A BIT TALLER!

The boys in blue

But in 1966, ten pitch-invaders went quite frantic. They were all sporting blue – two because they were Everton fans, and the other eight because they were policemen!

When the Everton fans ran on to the Wembley pitch to celebrate their side scoring against Sheffield Wednesday, the police team swung into action. One of them dived for a fan and missed, the second brought him down with a rugby tackle and the other six carted him off (feeling blue, no doubt).

Where are the workers?

It's not only fans who go frantic. In 1946 the Government went wild after a huge crowd of over 80,000 turned up to watch the semi-final replay between Derby County and Birmingham City. Why? Because it was held on a Wednesday afternoon – and most of the crowd were supposed to be at work! Soon after, mid-week afternoon matches were banned.

YES, SIR, I AM WORKING...

Where are the spectators?

Crowds weren't always as big as expected. In 1909 Notts County thought they'd get a poor crowd playing their first-round tie right next door to their more popular neighbours Notts Forest, so they sold home advantage to their opponents, Bradford City, for £1,000. It was rotten deal for both clubs. Bradford won the game 4-2 but the gate money was less than the £1,000 they'd paid out!

Where's the money?

Even when a big crowd does turn up it's not always good news. Cardiff City took record gate money when they met Queens Park Rangers in the FA Cup third round in 1990 but didn't get to keep a penny of it – because thieves broke in and stole the lot. Cardiff were frantic!

THE NOT ONLY THE MOST WITTY BUT ALSO THE MOST WRONG CROWD BANNER AWARD...

Fans of Queens Park Rangers. With their star player Tony Currie up against Tottenham Hotspur's ace Glenn Hoddle in the 1982 Cup Final, they made a banner supporting their man. It read:

CURRIE GIVES HODDLE THE RUNS!

Sadly, they got it wrong. After a 1-1 draw, Spurs won the replay 1-0 ... their goal scored by Hoddle from a penalty given away ... by Currie.

Darwen's dilemma

Before TV came along fans weren't able to sit on a comfy sofa and watch their team, they had to go to the match. But in 1879 it was only due to their fans that the *team* got to the match!

The team was Darwen, in Lancashire. The lively Lancastrians had fought their way through to a tie against the mighty Old Etonians in the quarter-finals of the FA Cup ... and that was the problem. The FA rules said that every match from the quarter-finals onwards had to be played at Kennington Oval, in London. But Darwen couldn't afford the fares. To get their whole team to London and back was going to cost a massive ... £31!

That may not sound much, but in 1880 for £31 you could...

more. Full time! Again the two captains had a quick discussion:

HOW ABOUT PLAYING EXTRA TIME?

WE'VE GOT TO. THIS IS A REPLAY. IT'S IN THE RULES DON'T Y'KNOW

But after an extra 30 minutes the score was still 2-2, which meant … yes, another collection and another round trip to London!

It was the final time. Suffering from train-lag, the exhausted Darwen team lost 6-2 and went out of the FA Cup (which Old Etonians went on to win). The FA took the hint, though. From then on, the rotten ground rule was scrapped to give non-London teams a fairer chance.

THE MOST TRAVELLED BUT NOWHERE NEAR BROKE AWARD…

Darwen. After all their collections and journeys, Darwen got back home to discover that they'd made a profit of over £56!

OOOH, PERHAPS WE SHOULD DO THIS AGAIN?

Round the grounds

Test your knockout know-it-all dad (or mum). What have the following clubs got in common?

> ## SURREY CRICKET CLUB

> ## MANCHESTER ATHLETIC CLUB

> ## EVERTON FOOTBALL CLUB

Answer: They've all had the FA Cup Final played on their grounds.

In fact before the FA Cup Final gained its permanent home at Wembley Stadium in 1923, it had been played on the grounds of seven other clubs…

- Kennington Oval (1872, 1874–92). Still the home of Surrey Cricket Club, the Oval staged 20 of the first 21 finals. When crowds started getting too colossal football was hit for six.

- Lillie Bridge, London (1873). This was the venue chosen by the Wanderers the year they were allowed to play the Final where they liked. The home of an Amateur Athletic Club, it was never used again for the knockout final and has since been knocked-down.

- Manchester (1893). Not Old Trafford, but a place called Fallowfield used by the Manchester Athletic Club. The Final stayed there just once, then sprinted off to...

- Goodison Park, Liverpool (1894), the home of Everton FC – and the first time in the 23 years it had been going that the FA Cup Final had been played on the ground of a football club! It didn't last. After one year it was back down to London again, and another non-footballing venue...

- Crystal Palace (1895–1914) which was *not* the home of the present-day Crystal Palace FC! It was a huge grassy area which Londoners went to for a day out. In fact one of the reasons FA Cup Finals kicked off at 3 p.m. or later was to give the spectators time to polish off their picnic! Although the crowds were truly colossal (120,081 in 1913), many of the spectators had to watch from a high bank 50 metres from the pitch. They'd only catch a glimpse of the ball if it was booted in the air!

- Old Trafford, Manchester (1915). Home of Manchester United. World War One had started and Crystal Palace was being used as a war depot (in other words ... it had been turned into a home for an arsenal!).
- Stamford Bridge, London (1920–22). Chelsea FC's ground. It was "smaller" (only 70,000 could get in!) but everybody could see.

At least they could see if they got in. That was the problem. The FA wanted a bigger venue for their big final so that a bigger crowd could watch it in comfort. After three years at Stamford Bridge, they found it. A ground that suited them – well, down to the ground.

So, in 1923, the FA Cup Final moved to a new stadium that had just been built at a place called Wembley – to be rewarded with a *much* bigger crowd...

PHENOMENAL FA CUP FINALS: 1923 BOLTON WANDERERS V. WEST HAM UNITED

Of all the phenomenal FA Cup Finals this was the most phenomenally frantic of the lot.

Here is the *Daily Mirror* newspaper headline the next day. Can you fill in the two gaps?

The Daily Mirror

_____ v _____ : Wembley's first Cup Final

Answer: Not Bolton Wanderers v. West Ham United, but "Police v. Crowd"!

Attracted by press advertisements for wonderful Wembley, over 200,000 people turned up. Some had tickets and some paid at the gate. But some didn't have tickets and climbed over the gate instead, while some knocked the gates down so that others didn't even have to climb over them!

ARE WE NEAR THE GATES?

VERY, YOU'RE STANDING ON THEM!

The result was that at 3 o'clock, kick-off time, out on the pitch were:
- 1 referee
- 2 linesmen

45

- 22 players

- 100,000 spectators

WHERE'S THE BALL?

WHERE'S THE PITCH?

- lots of police on brownie-coloured horses
- one policeman, George Scorey, on a white horse, Billy.

Only through steady pushing by the police horses was the crowd finally moved back to the touchlines so that, 45 minutes late and with spectators still lining the pitch, the game began.

THE MOST PHENOMENALLY FAMOUS NON-WHITE WHITE HORSE AWARD...

Billy the police horse, whose colouring caused 1923 to go down in history as "The White Horse Final". Except that he wasn't really white. It was a dull day and Billy had come out lighter in the newspapers than he really was because the photographs had been over-exposed to make them clearer. So 1923 should really have been called "The Dirty Grey Horse Final".

Bolton won the game 2-0. Their first goal, the first goal ever scored at Wembley, was as phenomenally frantic as the occasion...

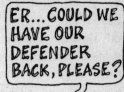

- Two minutes gone. The ball goes out of play and disappears into the crowd.
- West Ham defender Jack Tresadern dives into the crowd to fetch it.
- The ball is thrown out – but Tresadern isn't!
- Bolton take the throw, the ball's crossed into the West Ham area, and Bolton's David Jack scores!

Then, just eight minutes into the second half...

- Bolton's Ted Vizard dribbles down the wing.
- He knocks the ball out of play (claim West Ham) – but a spectator passes it back to him!
- Vizard runs on and crosses the ball.
- John Smith of Bolton whacks it into the West Ham goal – but it rockets straight back out again!

Here's what was said to the referee straight afterwards. Which of the statements did he agree with?

a) West Ham: "It hit the post, ref!"

b) Bolton: "It hit the spectators behind the net, ref!"

c) West Ham: "This is ridiculous. Abandon the game, ref!"

d) Bolton: "We're doing fine, ref. We'll play until dark to finish the game if necessary."

Answers: b) and **d)**. The referee gave the goal, and kept the match going until the end to leave Bolton Wanderers the winners of the first Wembley final by two goals to nil.

 THE MOST PHENOMENALLY BORING QUESTION AWARD...

PC George Scorey's girlfriend, who asked, when the policeman got home after he'd tucked his horse Billy up for the night,

WHAT KIND OF DAY DID YOU HAVE?

 THE MOST PHENOMENALLY BORING ANSWER TO A PHENOMENALLY BORING QUESTION AWARD...

PC George Scorey, who replied,

 **JUST ORDINARY, LASS**

CUP CRAFTINESS AND
TROPHY TRICKERY

The FA Cup wasn't always seen as one of the most important competitions around. Teams would sometimes pull out for the most curious reasons...

- In 1880 Aston Villa pulled out of their second-round tie against Oxford University and played a Birmingham Senior Cup match instead!

- In 1923 Bournemouth pulled out because they weren't allowed to go straight into the first round even though they'd just been elected to the League. At least, that was their story. They could have been scared of meeting their opponents – the Portsea Gas Company!

They were the exceptions, though. Soon the FA Cup became a trophy teams wanted to win. If they could do it with tricky play, fine. But if they couldn't, trickery of a different sort was always worth a try.

Do you have what it takes to get your hands on the Cup? Try this tricky round-by-round quiz. Get an answer right and you're through to the next round. Get it wrong and you're knocked out. But be warned – the questions are tricky!

First round In 1932 Brighton had to play in the first qualifying round, even though they were a League team. Were they the victims of trickery? YES or NO?

Second round In 1999–2000, Darlington lost in the second round but still managed to reach the third round. Did they manage it by trickery? YES or NO?

Third round In 1939, non-league Scarborough reached the third round claiming they'd benefited from some pre-match training trickery. What was it?
a) Eating huge steak dinners.
b) Knocking back drinks of eggs mixed with rum.
c) Soaking in seaweed.

Fourth round During the draw for the fourth round of the 1974–5 competition, Leeds were drawn at home. The next ball out of the bag was West Ham's – but they didn't go on to play star-studded Leeds in the next round. Was it trickery? YES or NO?

Fifth round In 1945–6, Bradford Park Avenue reached the fifth round even though they'd lost 1-3 at home to Manchester City in the fourth round. Was it trickery? YES or NO?

Sixth round Arsenal reached the sixth round in 1999 after beating Sheffield United 2-1. In that match, Sheffield United had kicked the ball out to let an injured player receive treatment. But when the throw was taken, instead of the ball being given back to Sheffield, a move began and Marc Overmars scored for Arsenal. Trickery? YES or NO?

SPLOSH!
SPLOSH!
SPLOSH!

Semi-final In the 1947 semi-final, Charlton Athletic goalkeeper Sam Bartram played the whole game with a hot soggy bandage under his jumper. Trickery? YES or NO?

Final In 1888, Preston North End asked if they could be photographed with the FA Cup. Were they being tricky? YES or NO?

WE WERE JUST WONDERING IF WE COULD HAVE A PHOTO OF US AND THE CUP... ER... JUST FOR OUR WIVES, YOU KNOW?

Answers:

First round – NO They'd scored an own goal by forgetting to claim their right to join the competition in the first round proper! In the end, they played 11 matches and reached the fifth round. (In 1983, as a First Division side, they played five games fewer and reached the final.)

Second round – NO Darlington were drawn as "lucky second-round losers" to go through to the third round in place of Manchester United, who'd withdrawn to play in the first-ever FIFA World Club Championship. Darlington's luck ran out at once. They lost in the third round as well.

Third round – c) Scarborough claimed that regular seaweed baths stopped their team from feeling all washed-up. A slap-up steak dinner and drinks of eggs and rum was the trick tried by non-league Kings Lynn before they played Southend United in 1968. Sadly, they ended up like the eggs: badly beaten! Southend won 9-0.

Fourth round – NO It was clumsiness. West Ham's ball was dropped on the floor, chased, picked up – then put back in the bag again! New opponents for Leeds were drawn ... and West Ham ended up with a home game instead, then went on to win the Cup!

Fifth round – NO In 1945–6 the rounds were played over two legs. Bradford Park Avenue lost at home 1-3, but won away 8-2 to go through 9-3 on aggregate.

Sixth round – officially, NO ... but everybody agreed, YES! NO, because the referee gave a goal since no laws had been broken. But YES because the move broke the unwritten rule that a team who sportingly halt the game should be given the ball back again. After the match, won by Arsenal 2-1, they acknowledged the trickiness of what happened and offered to replay the game. They did, Arsenal won 2-1 again ... and Overmars scored again but more fairly this time!

HOLD ON! THERE'LL HAVE TO BE ANOTHER REPLAY. HE SCORED WHEN I WASN'T LOOKING!

Semi-final – NO Bartram had been suffering from food poisoning so he wound the bandage round his tum to make him feel better. It did, too. Charlton won 4-0 and went on to lift the Cup.

Final – YES They wanted to demoralize their opponents, West Bromwich Albion, by being photographed with the cup *before* the game, while their kit was still clean! The referee refused – and Preston lost.

Curses! Will we never win?

Sometimes the only way to fight trickery is with a bit more trickery, as Derby County did in 1946. Their problem was over 50 years old, dating back to 1895 when they were looking for a piece of land...

The Romanies left and the ground was built. And how did Derby do in the years that followed? Phenomenally badly!

1896 LOST IN SEMI-FINAL

1897 LOST IN SEMI-FINAL

1898 LOST IN FINAL, 3-1 TO NOTTINGHAM FOREST

1899 LOST IN FINAL, 4-1 TO SHEFFIELD UNITED

1902 LOST IN SEMI-FINAL

1903 LOST IN FINAL, BY A RECORD 6-0 TO BURY!

BEAT'EM? WE BURY-ED'EM!

1909 LOST IN SEMI-FINAL

1923 LOST IN SEMI-FINAL

1933 LOST IN SEMI-FINAL

CURSES! WILL WE NEVER WIN THE CUP?

So when they reached the 1946 FA Cup Final, desperate Derby decided it was time to do something about this curse. Off went their captain, Jack Nicholas, to find a Romany. He crossed her palm with silver, she lifted the curse ... and Derby whacked Charlton 4-1 to win the FA Cup for the first time in their history!

WHEN YOU SAID SILVER I WAS KIND OF HOPING 10p WOULD BE ENOUGH!

Goalie games

Goalkeepers are the trickiest players in the game. They'll try anything to keep the ball out of their net...

• In the 1922 Final, Huddersfield were awarded a penalty against Preston. Time for trickery from Huddersfield goalie James Mitchell. As the penalty-taker ran in, Mitchell started jumping up and down and waving his arms to try and put him off.

Mitchell was like an excited monkey on a stick awaiting the offer of a bag of peanuts

It didn't work, either. The penalty was scored to give Huddersfield a 1-0 win ... and the following season goalkeepers facing penalties were banned from moving about until the ball was kicked (a rule which stayed until 1998).

● As for Manchester United goalkeeper Gary Bailey, his trickery was nothing less than magic! In his first three Wembley finals he'd let in seven goals, including a couple in the 2-2 draw with Brighton in the 1983 Final. So for the replay, South African-born Bailey brought his muti along to help him. Who or what was it? (Clue: he took his case to a witch-doctor.)

Answer: A muti is a magic sign. Bailey tied ribbons in his team's colours to his goalpost and fixed a padlock and key to the net ... and with Gary's guarded goal, Manchester United won 4-0.

● Some spectators might have thought that West Bromwich Albion goalkeeper Jim Sanders was being tricky during the 1954 Cup Final against Preston. With Preston 2-1 ahead, West Bromwich were awarded a penalty. Sanders immediately turned round to face the other way and hugged his goalpost. Was he trying a bit of magic? No, he was just too frightened to watch – and only looked up again when the roar of the crowd told him his team had scored. Mind you, when West Brom scored again to win 3-2 he thought *that* was magic!

- Another goalkeeper who didn't know where to look was Billy Bly of non-league side Weymouth. When their game against Preston was abandoned after 14 minutes because of thick fog, both teams trooped back to the dressing rooms. It was only some while later that the Weymouth manager, Frank O'Farrell, realized that Bly wasn't in there with them. O'Farrell looked everywhere until, finally, he went back out on to the pitch – and found Bly still pacing up and down in his goal! "I thought we were putting Preston under a lot of pressure at the other end" was his explanation!

WHAT'S HAPPENING? HAVE I MIST ANYTHING?

PHENOMENAL FA CUP FINALS: 1927 ARSENAL V. CARDIFF CITY...AND 1934 MANCHESTER CITY V. PORTSMOUTH

Or ... a tale of two more goalkeepers. So, grab your gloves, put on your bright new jersey, and get between the sticks. You're about to find out what it's like to be a goalkeeper in an FA Cup Final!

1927 In goal for Arsenal ... Dan Lewis, full of experience.

1934 In goal for Manchester City ... Frank Swift, inexperienced and only 19 years old.

1927 The game begins. It's evenly balanced. The FA Cup has never been taken out of England, but Cardiff are hoping to do the trick and carry it home with them to Wales. Lewis is aiming to stop them – after all, he *is* an international goalkeeper.
1934 The game begins. Swift is still a bag of nerves, even though the Manchester City captain, Sam Cowan, spent the whole evening before telling him stories to try and take his mind off the game.
1927 Lewis hasn't had much to worry about. Arsenal are getting on top and winning corners. By the end of the game they'll have beaten Cardiff 8-0 ... on corners...

1934 26 minutes: Rutherford of Portsmouth hits a powerful shot. Swift gets his hand to the ball – but can't stop it! His team are 1-0 down.

1927 Half-time. It's been all Arsenal, but they haven't scored and it's still 0-0. Jimmy McEwan, the man in charge of their dressing room, is confident though. He's got the champagne  all ready. As for Dan Lewis, he's had so little to do his nice new goalkeeping jersey is still as shiny as when he put it on.

IF WE DON'T WIN I WON'T SPEAK TO MYSELF FOR A WEEK!

1934 Half-time. Swift is swearing. He's blaming himself for letting in the goal, saying he should have stopped it, boo-hoo. Frank Tilson, Manchester City's centre-forward, tells him, "Don't worry, son. I'm going to score two in the second half!"

1927 73 minutes. Still 0-0, and the Lewis jersey is still unmuddied.

1934 73 minutes. 1-1! Manchester City have hit an equalizer. And who's scored it? As good as his word, it's Frank Tilson! Swift starts sweating.

1927 74 minutes. Hugh Ferguson of Cardiff has a shot, but it's a soft one. It trickles all along the ground towards Dan Lewis, who...

● goes down on one knee...
● gathers it into his arms and

presses it against his shiny new jersey…

- only for the ball to slide off his new jersey, out of his arms and spin towards the line!
- With a couple of Cardiff players rushing in, Lewis makes a desperate grab for it…
- but can only push the ball *over* the line! Cardiff are 1-0 ahead.

1934 87 minutes. Tilson scores again! It's 2-1 to Manchester City with only three minutes to go. Now Swift is really sweating.

1927 Full-time. Arsenal have lost, 1-0.

1934 Behind his goal, a photographer is making Swift more and more anxious by telling him how long there is to go. "Only fifty seconds … forty … thirty…" so that when the referee finally does blow his whistle the relief is so great that Swift promptly faints!

1927 Lewis trudges miserably up the Wembley steps to receive his loser's medal from King George V.

1934 Swift has to be helped up the Wembley steps to receive his winner's medal from King George V.

1927 and after The Arsenal players get back to the dressing room to discover that their kit man, Jimmy McEwan couldn't bear the thought of his team having to force themselves to drink the champagne he'd brought – so he's drunk it all himself! As for Dan Lewis, he never lives down his terrible mistake, always being known as the goalkeeper who allowed the FA Cup out of England. But he goes on to play more games for Arsenal, and for his country – Wales!

1934 and after Frank Swift is always remembered as the goalkeeper who fainted, but he grew in confidence and became an England international, playing for his country 19 times.

THE MOST-WASHED GOALKEEPER'S JERSEY AWARD...

Every Arsenal goalkeeper's jersey following the 1927 FA Cup Final. Disastrous Dan Lewis's slippery jersey began an Arsenal tradition. From then on, none of their goalkeepers has played in a new jersey unless it's been washed to take the shine off it.

FEE-FI-FO-FUM! FA CUP GIANT-KILLERS

The FA Cup has been providing shock results ever since dashing Darwen took the train down to London in 1879 and steamed into the puffing Old Etonians. Darwen didn't actually beat their opponents (getting a draw was shocking enough), but plenty of smaller teams have done just that.

Before we tell their triumphant tales, can you sort out the giant-killers from the giants? Fit these five teams into the gaps in the newspaper cuttings…

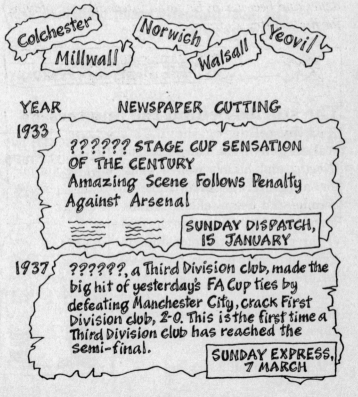

Colchester
Norwich
Yeovil
Millwall
Walsall

YEAR	NEWSPAPER CUTTING
1933	?????? STAGE CUP SENSATION OF THE CENTURY Amazing Scene Follows Penalty Against Arsenal SUNDAY DISPATCH, 15 JANUARY
1937	??????, a Third Division club, made the big hit of yesterday's FA Cup ties by defeating Manchester City, crack First Division club, 2-0. This is the first time a Third Division club has reached the semi-final. SUNDAY EXPRESS, 7 MARCH

1949
EGGS AND SHERRY TEAM STILL IN THE CUP
?????'s victory is the toast of the West

NEWS OF THE WORLD, 30 JANUARY

1959
Mac's Marvels march on! All hell broke loose at ????? last night when the golden boot of Terry Bly flattened Spurs.

DAILY HERALD, 19 FEBRUARY

1971
The most fantastic result you'll ever see: ?????? 3 LEEDS 2

THE PEOPLE, 14 FEBRUARY

The stories behind the answers

1933 Walsall

Walsall were in the Third Division (North) and hadn't won a game for a month. Arsenal were to become the team of the 1930s. They were on their way to the first of three league championships in a row and their players had cost a fortune. Everything about them was expensive. At a total price of £87, their football boots had cost more than the whole Walsall team!

Result: Walsall 2 Arsenal 0

I'M WORTH TWO OF YOUR STUDS, MATE

It was a rough game, with arrogant Arsenal being roughed up non-stop by wild Walsall.

"They were more like steamrollers than footballers," said the Arsenal left-winger Cliff Bastin afterwards.

ER... STRETCHER, PLEASE

This may explain why so much flattening went on. Walsall's centre-forward Gilbert Alsop put his team ahead in the second half. Shortly after, he was flattened by Arsenal full-back Tommy Black. Alsop's team-mates rushed up and tried to flatten Black (and turn him black and blue). The Arsenal players dived in to try to flatten the Walsall players. When the dust settled the referee awarded a penalty to Walsall for Black's foul, Sheppard scored – and Arsenal were flat out.

THE BEST PRESERVED WALSALL FOOTBALL AWARD...

The ball used in the Arsenal v. Walsall match. It has a silver medallion attached to it commemorating Walsall's victory and lives in the club's trophy room.

1937 Millwall

First Division sides were expected to fire their way to the FA Cup Final. Second Division sides were expected to stagger their way to the semi-finals if they were lucky. Third Division sides were expected to get thumped.

But in 1937 it was Millwall, from the Third Division (South) who did the thumping. Nicknamed "The Lions", and their ground "The Den", they chewed up three First Division teams in succession.

ER...GULP! NICE PUSSY...

The third was Manchester City. With Millwall ahead 1-0, over came the ball ... out swooped the Manchester City goalkeeper ... only to miss it, allowing Mangall of Millwall to score with a simple header. And who was the swooping City goalkeeper? None other than 1934 Cup-winner, fainting Frank Swift!

Result: Millwall 2 Manchester City 0

That's where it ended for Millwall. They were beaten in the semi-finals by Sunderland. But they'd made history.

1949 Yeovil

Southern League team Yeovil Town had a secret training diet of glucose and sherry, mixed with eggs, and played on a sloping pitch. As their opponents – top First Division side, Sunderland – found out, this was no yolk!

The small stadium was packed with spectators and newspaper reporters. It normally only had a small grandstand, but Yeovil had brought in more seats especially for the game. What were they made from?

a) metal scaffolding

b) beer crates

c) junior school desks

Answer: b) and **c)** The proper metal scaffolding was too expensive, so extra seats for spectators were made out of beer crates (and Yeovil charged 37p to sit on them instead of the usual 10p). The school desks were put along the touchline and the newspaper reporters sat at them with their knees up under their chins.

WRITE OUT ONE THOUSAND TIMES, YEOVIL FOR THE CUP!

They all saw an amazing game. Yeovil took the lead, Sunderland equalized, only for Yeovil to go 2-1 ahead with 15 minutes to go. How did Yeovil manage to hang on? Frantically, that's how!

● They'd frantically whack the ball down the slope to the Sunderland end.

- Better still, they'd frantically whack the ball into the stand.
- Even better still, they'd frantically whack the ball out of the ground!

As this went on, Sunderland's star striker, Len Shackleton, had a quick word with their player-manager, Alec Stock:

Yeovil won the game and in the next round went to Old Trafford to play Manchester United. Did the egg diet work? No. They spent the whole match scrambling around while United whisked in goals galore to win 8-0.

1959 Norwich

After Millwall, another couple of Third Division sides had managed to reach the semi-finals: Port Vale in 1954 and York City in 1955. In later years they were followed by Crystal Palace (1976), Plymouth Argyle (1984) and Chesterfield (in 1997, by which time the old Third Division had become the new Second Division).

But none have come closer to reaching Wembley than Norwich City did in 1959. On the way they beat three First Division sides before the semi-finals...

ROUND 3: Manchester United, 3-0
ROUND 5: Tottenham Hotspur, 1-0 after 1-1 draw
ROUND 6: Sheffield United, 3-2 after 1-1 draw

Ken Nethercott, the Norwich goalkeeper, was one of their heroes. After the Manchester United game he said, "I've never had an easier afternoon in my life!" He didn't say the same after the first game against Sheffield United, though – because mid-way through he dislocated his shoulder. He couldn't use his right arm. Talk about a hand-icap!

But this was in the days before substitutes. So Nethercott played on, using his good arm and his chest to make saves – and Norwich forced a replay, which they won. They were in the semi-finals!

Their opponents were Luton Town, then a First Division side. The first game was drawn, 1-1. It was on to a replay. Luton went ahead, 1-0. Norwich counter-attacked. A shot whistled towards the Luton net … and was kicked off the line! Luton had won the game (but went on to lose the Final) and Norwich were out.

I'VE NEVER SEEN SO MANY GROWN MEN CRYING

NORWICH CAPTAIN, RON ASHMAN

A good side has got to have a confident manager, right? One who believes his team can beat any side, however big?

THE LEAST CONFIDENT GIANT-KILLER'S MANAGER AWARD...

Dick Graham, manager of Colchester. Before they played Leeds, he said, "If my team win I'll climb the walls of Colchester Castle."

Graham had good reason to say what he did. Colchester were half-way down the Fourth Division. Leeds were 74 places higher, on top of the First Division. Leeds were stuffed with internationals. Colchester were just going to get stuffed. But it didn't work out that way...

18 MINS: COLCHESTER 1 LEEDS 0

24 MINS: COLCHESTER 2 LEEDS 0

54 MINS: COLCHESTER 3 LEEDS 0

60 MINS: COLCHESTER 3 LEEDS 1

73 MINS: COLCHESTER 3 LEEDS 2

90 MINS: GAME OVER - WITH LEEDS LOOKING LIKE TURKEYS AND COLCHESTER THINKING IT'S STILL CHRISTMAS!

THE AS-GOOD-AS-HIS-WORD MANAGER'S AWARD...

Dick Graham, manager of Colchester. After they'd beaten Leeds, he did exactly what he'd said he'd do and climbed the walls of Colchester Castle – all 14–15 metres of it.

For the next round, Dick Graham didn't say a word. Maybe that's where he went wrong. His team went to Everton and lost 5-0!

Magic Moments and Golden Goals

The history of the FA Cup is littered with magic moments and golden goals. What makes a moment magic or a goal golden? It's often something to do with being unexpected.

- Like the magic moment in 1873 when Lord Kinnaird (the standing-on-his-head superstar of Wanderers and Old Etonians) was driving to the Cup Final in his carriage and was spotted by the crowd. Was he mobbed by his supporters or pelted by rival fans? Neither. The crowds were so fond of the lively Lord that they unhitched the horses from his carriage and pulled it all the way to the match themselves!

- Or ... like the golden goal scored in the 1878 FA Cup Final by the Royal Engineers. Playing the kick-and-rush tactics of the time, the whole team surged after the ball in a pack and just kept on

72

running until they discovered they were in their opponent's goal – with nobody having any idea who'd got the final touch! It's the only goal in the history of the FA Cup Final that hasn't got a goalscorer.

The unexpected quiz

So expect the unexpected with the difficult dozen in this quiz as you try to sort out the golden goals from what happened next!

1 It's 1894 and Reading have a qualifying match coming up against Southampton St Mary's. They desperately need their part-time star striker, a soldier named Jimmy Stewart. Unfortunately, Stewart is in the guardhouse. What happens next?

a) He escapes and plays the whole game.

b) He escapes, only to be recaptured in the middle of the match.

c) A Reading official tries to bribe a guard and gets arrested too.

2 It's 1913, and the night before the final between Aston Villa and Sunderland. Tucked up in bed, Villa player Clem Stephenson dreams that his team will win 1-0 with a headed goal. Next day, with only 15 minutes to go, his team-mate Tommy Barber leaps into the air and heads the ball. Golden Goal? YES or NO?

3 It's 1908 and Wolverhampton Wanderers are playing Newcastle United in the Cup Final. The Reverend Kenneth Hunt turns up in the Wolverhampton dressing room. What happens next?
a) He gets changed into his Wolves football kit.
b) He says special prayers for a Wolves victory.
c) He tells them what tactics to use.

4 It's 1902, Derby County are playing Lincoln City in a cup-tie, and it's Derby to kick off. The moment they do, a bunch of their players surround the ball so that none of the Lincoln team can get near it. When they get near the Lincoln goal they all jump to one side and one of their players bangs it into the net! Golden goal? YES or NO?

5 It's 1970 and full-time in the FA Cup Final replay between Chelsea and Leeds United. Chelsea have won and David Webb, scorer of the winning goal, swaps shirts with a Leeds player. What happens next?

a) He's mistaken for a Leeds player and has his winner's medal stolen by Chelsea fans.

b) He's mistaken for a Leeds player and gets a loser's medal.

c) He's mistaken for a Leeds player and isn't allowed up to get a medal at all.

6 It's 1932. Arsenal are playing Newcastle and winning 1-0 when Newcastle forward, Jimmy Richardson, chases after a pass. He doesn't get to it before the ball goes over the touchline, but hooks it across anyway. His team-mate Jack Allen pops it into the net. Golden Goal? YES or NO?

7 It's 1965, and Wigan Athletic are playing Doncaster Rovers in a first round replay when Wigan's H. (Harry) Lyon is carried off with an agonizing ankle injury. In the dressing room the Wigan trainer fills Lyon up with whisky and pain-killing tablets. What happens next?

a) Lyon returns to the pitch and scores a hat-trick.

b) Lyon returns to the pitch only to get sent off again for being drunk.

c) Lyon returns to the pitch but starts kicking the wrong way.

8 It's 1957 and Manchester United are playing Bolton Wanderers in the Final. With Bolton one-nil up, United's goalkeeper Harry Gregg saves a fierce shot by pushing it up into the air. As it comes down again, Bolton's Nat Lofthouse charges in and knocks Gregg and the ball into the net. Golden Goal? YES or NO?

9 It's 1930, and Arsenal are playing Huddersfield Town at Wembley. Suddenly there's a terrific roar. What happens next?

a) Arsenal score.

b) Huddersfield score.

c) Neither of them score.

10 It's the 1920 Cup Final between Aston Villa and Huddersfield Town. Over comes a corner. Villa's Billy Kirton jumps with a group of other players – and the ball flies into the Huddersfield net for the only goal of the game. Does Kirton think he's scored a golden goal? YES or NO?

11 It's 1974 and Liverpool have just beaten Newcastle United 3-0 in the Final. Two fans run on to the Wembley pitch and straight up to the revered Liverpool manager, Bill Shankly. What happens next?

a) They kiss his feet.

b) They kiss his backside.

c) They kiss his lips.

YOU'LL NEVER WALK ALONE

12 It's the 1983 Final between Manchester United and Brighton Hove Albion. It's 2-2 and in the last minute of the game Gordon Smith, scorer of Brighton's first goal, finds himself in front of the Manchester goal with only their keeper to beat. On the radio the commentator screams, "And Smith must score…!" Golden Goal? YES or NO?

Answers:

BYE! GOOD LUCK WITH THE GAME

1a) Reading's secretary, Harold Walker, turned up at the jail with some bottles of whisky, got Stewart's guard drunk, then talked him into letting his prisoner out for the afternoon! When Southampton found out they lodged a protest. It was turned down. Stewart was a registered Reading player and there were no rules saying he couldn't be a prisoner as well. What had made Southampton sore was that Stewart had scored the winning goal. How? With a shot on the run, of course!

2 YES And Aston Villa win 1-0. What you would call a dream come true!

3a) Although he probably did **b)**, and might have done **c)** as well. Kenneth Hunt was a Wolves player as well as an ordained minister. He was an amateur international and his goal for Wolves in their 3-1 win was the last goal scored by an amateur in the Cup Final. Afterwards, Hunt said of their surprise victory – Newcastle were a First Division side and Wolves in the Second Division – "Our win was due to dash, quick tackling and direct methods". In other words, Newcastle didn't have a prayer!

HOLY SMOKE!

4 YES Unlike he would nowadays, the referee didn't award Lincoln a free-kick for obstruction. He couldn't – the rule wasn't invented until 1948.

5c) An official stops Webb going up to collect his medal with the rest of the Chelsea team because he thinks he's a Leeds player. Webb had to wait until he returned to the dressing room before he got his medal!

YOU CAN'T COME IN HERE, THIS IS THE CHELSEA DRESSING ROOM

THIS IS THE LAST TIME I SWAP SHIRTS

6 YES! It's one of the most famous Cup Final goals ever because it was the first that TV and newspaper pictures "proved" should never have been allowed. But it was, and Newcastle went on to score again and win the match 2-1.

7a) Wigan win 3-1 as Lyon scores with two headers … and a goal from his badly injured foot!

8 YES Shoulder-charging the goalkeeper was (and still is) allowed, and that's what the referee decided Lofthouse had done.

I USED TO PRAY QUIETLY– THIS WAS AT ONE STAGE WHEN THE PRESS SAID NAT WAS GOING TO RETIRE – PLEASE GOD, DON'T LET HIM RETIRE UNTIL I GET ONE SMACK AT HIM

HARRY GREGG

9c) The roar came from the engines of the massive German airship Graf Zeppelin as it hovered over the stadium. After dipping its nose in salute to King George V it then moved on.

10 NO He hasn't got a clue who's scored. He only finds out it was him when the referee tells him – after the match is over!

11a) It was the last chance they had. A few weeks later, Shankly announced his retirement. He was going to put his feet up!

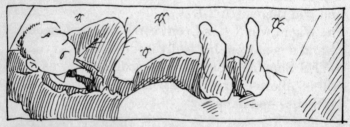

12 NO Smith's shot is saved, the match is drawn, and Manchester United win the replay 4-0. Brighton's supporters never forget Smith's sitter and even call their own magazine: *And Smith Must Score*.

PHENOMENAL FA CUP FINALS: 1953 BLACKPOOL V. BOLTON WANDERERS

Cup-winners regularly gasp when they're clutching their medal that the whole experience feels like a fairy tale. Well, if ever an FA Cup Final could be said to have a fairy-tale ending, this was it…

*O*nce upon a time, 1953 to be exact, there were two footballers. They were both named Stanley and they lived in a land of sand called Blackpool.

One was named Stanley Matthews. He was a wizard. "Wizard of Dribble", they called him because he had twinkling toes and could do magical things with a football.

The other was named Stanley Mortensen. He wasn't called anything special, just "Stan" – but not because he just used to Stan-d around! He had magical gifts, too. He could take one of Stanley's passes and turn it into a goal!

Stan and Stanley had both had wonderful careers. They'd both worked their magic many times for England. But one thing was missing, and causing them great sadness. "If I could only be granted an FA Cup-winner's medal," they both sighed, "then I would be truly happy!"

81

But Stanley and Stan were both getting old. Stan was 32 – and as for Stanley, he was 38! Everybody wondered if their magical gifts were fading. Could they still make wishes come true?

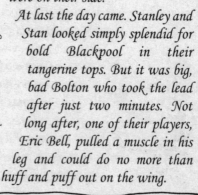

After all, they said, they'd had two wishes already. They'd had the first in the Cup Final of 1948, when bold Blackpool had played mean Manchester United, and that wish hadn't been granted. They'd lost 4-2.

Then they'd had their second wish in 1951, when brave Blackpool played nasty Newcastle. That wish hadn't been granted either. They'd lost 2-0.

Was this going to be their third and final wish? If Stanley and Stan couldn't work their magic against big, bad Bolton they might never get another chance. And so not only the citizens of Blackpool, but also citizens the length and breadth of the Queendom (except in big, bad Bolton, of course) were on their side.

At last the day came. Stanley and Stan looked simply splendid for bold Blackpool in their tangerine tops. But it was big, bad Bolton who took the lead after just two minutes. Not long after, one of their players, Eric Bell, pulled a muscle in his leg and could do no more than huff and puff out on the wing.

Bell's injury meant Bolton had to ring the changes. They shuffled their side around ... but after 35 minutes up popped Stan to score for brave Blackpool!

Back came Bolton – and scored again after 39 minutes. On into the second half they went – and after 55 minutes big, bad Bolton's battling Bell scored another! Bolton 3, Blackpool 1. Everywhere wails of woe were waiting to be wept (except in big, bad Bolton of course).

And then Stanley and Stan had their magic spell.

After 68 minutes, Stan stabbed the ball home after the Bolton goalkeeper's big, bad bumble had dropped it at his feet. Then, with just a minute left to play, bonny Blackpool won a free kick ... and up stepped Stan to smash a smasher straight into big, bad Bolton's net. Bolton 3, Blackpool 3!

Into injury time. Stanley got the ball out on the wing. Big, bad Bolton's full-back, Banks, had been crippled by cruel cramp. Stanley strode past him. The other desperate defenders, wearied by Stanley's wonderful weaving, struggled to stop him. But, mesmerizingly and magically, Stanley dribbled on ... before sliding a cracking cross into the perfect path of Perry who banged it in for brave Blackpool's phenomenal fourth! Bolton 3, Blackpool 4!

And so it was that Stan and Stanley won their medals. There was great rejoicing throughout the land (except in big, bad Bolton of course) and they both played happily ever after.

Well, that's the fairy-tale telling and it's true that the neutral supporters were pleased for Blackpool and for Stanley Matthews especially.

But they also had a lot of sympathy for Bolton Wanderers – who might have been big, but certainly weren't bad! Bell's injury had meant they'd played most of the game with ten men.

Stan Mortensen played happily for Blackpool, not for ever after, but for another six years, until he retired. Later he spent a couple of years as Blackpool manager, but they were anything but happy years: his team was relegated and he was sacked.

Stanley Matthews didn't play for ever after either … but he got closer than anybody else has ever done or is ever likely to do! When he finally retired, still in the First Division with Stoke City, he was 50 years old!

He died in February 2000, but his name will live on as long as FA Cup Finals are remembered; the 1953 final has always been known as the "Matthews Final". Stanley knew the score though, and often said:

POOR STAN MORTENSEN. PEOPLE FORGET IT WAS HIM THAT SCORED A HAT-TRICK. IT SHOULD REALLY BE CALLED THE STAN MORTENSEN FINAL, YOU KNOW

THE LEAST GRATEFUL FORMER PLAYER AWARD...

Joe Smith, manager of Blackpool's winning side in 1953. He'd previously won a Cup-winner's medal as a player both in 1923 and 1926 – with Bolton!

Who scored?

Everybody knew Stanley Matthews ... but that wasn't the case for an Everton player in the 1966 FA Cup Final. Their striker, Mike Trebilcock, had only been with the club six months and had hardly played for the first team. So when he was chosen for the Final against Sheffield Wednesday it was such a big surprise his name wasn't even in the match programme – even though he ended up scoring two of Everton's goals in their 3-2 victory.

Whata loada rubbish!

Not every FA Cup Final is given a fairy-tale name, either. The 1960 final between Blackburn Rovers and Wolverhampton Wanderers, won 3-0 by Wolves, wasn't a good game. The crowd thought the referee had been too soft and Wolves' tackling too tough – so both were pelted with apple cores and orange peel as they came off and the match became known as "The Dustbin Final"!

THE WEMBLEY HOODOO

Bolton's brave Eric Bell wasn't the first player to be injured in a Cup Final. As early as 1878, a player named Kirkpatrick was hurt playing for the Wanderers in only the third Final ever staged, helping them to beat Royal Engineers 3-1.

As a newspaper reported at the time:

> Kirkpatrick fractured his left arm early in the game, but played on to the last

Was Kirkpatrick keen or krazy? Probably both. He was the Wanderers' goalkeeper!

There was a period starting in the 1950s when nearly every FA Cup Final saw somebody getting badly injured – and, as substitutes weren't allowed at that time, the crocked player (like battling Bell) was having to struggle on.

It became known as the "Wembley hoodoo" – because hoodoo means "bad luck", not because everybody was wondering, "Hoodoo you think will get injured today?"

Here's the tortuous timetable:

1952 After 30 minutes, Arsenal right-back Wally Barnes twists his knee as he turns to chase Newcastle's left-winger Bobby Mitchell. He has to go off. Arsenal lose 0-2.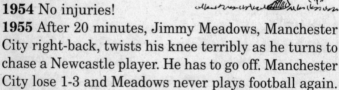

1953 After 15 minutes, Eric Bell of Bolton Wanderers pulls a muscle against Blackpool. He struggles through the rest of the game and even scores a goal, but Bolton lose 3-4.

1954 No injuries!

1955 After 20 minutes, Jimmy Meadows, Manchester City right-back, twists his knee terribly as he turns to chase a Newcastle player. He has to go off. Manchester City lose 1-3 and Meadows never plays football again.

> ## THE MOST TRICKY WEMBLEY WINGER AWARD...
>
> **Bobby Mitchell of Newcastle United**. Wally Barnes had twisted his knee chasing Mitchell in 1952. Meadows suffered the same kind of injury, only far worse, in 1955. And who was he turning to chase? Bobby Mitchell.

1956 After 75 minutes, Bert Trautmann, a German prisoner-of-war who stayed behind in England to become Manchester City's goalkeeper, is injured as he dives at the feet of Peter Murphy of Birmingham City. He plays on for the rest of the game, which Manchester City win 3-1. Afterwards Trautmann totters off to hospital for an X-ray. What did he discover he'd done?

Answer: He'd broken his neck! If he'd made one false move in the final 15 minutes he might have been dead.

1957 After six minutes, Ray Wood, Manchester United goalkeeper, catches a header from Peter McParland, Aston Villa forward. McParland doesn't stop running, but launches himself at Wood. A moment later Wood is on the ground with a broken cheekbone. (McParland? He's still on the field. He wasn't even booked.) Wood comes back to play on the wing for a while but Manchester United lose 1-2, with McParland scoring both Villa's goals.

1958 No injuries!
1959 After 30 minutes, Roy Dwight of Nottingham Forest breaks Luton Town hearts with a goal after ten minutes, then breaks his leg in a tackle with a

Luton defender. Forest hang on to win 2-1 with ten men.

1960 In the forty-second minute Dave Whelan of Blackburn Rovers breaks his leg tackling Norman Deeley of Wolverhampton Wanderers. Deeley goes on to score two goals as Blackburn lose 0-3. Whelan goes on to become a millionaire businessman after his injury forces him to retire. What you might call a lucky break?

1961 In the nineteenth minute Leicester City full-back Len Chalmers twists his knee and is forced to limp out to the wing. He can't Len-d much of a hand out there and Leicester lose

0-2 to Tottenham Hotspur (who become the first team in the 20th century to win the "double" of League Championship and FA Cup in the same season).

1962–64 No injuries. But the horrible hoodoo is only having a holiday and soon it's back…

1965 Gerry Byrne of Liverpool breaks three things in one match!

1 A record. His injury, after just three minutes, is the quickest of all the Wembley hoodoo years.

2 His collarbone. But he plays on for the remaining 87 minutes – and, as if that isn't enough, Byrne has to burn up the pitch for another 30 minutes when the game goes into extra time! It's worth it, though. Liverpool collar the Cup, beating Leeds United 2-1.

3 Another record. He's the last player to be injured without a substitute being available to replace him. The following season the FA allow one substitute to come on – but only for an injured player.

Injury time!

Snap to it! What did each member of this hat-trick of phenomenal FA Cup performers break?

1 Reg Cutler (Bournemouth), when he was brought to a sudden halt during the fourth-round tie against Wolverhampton Wanderers in 1957. (Cracking clue: If it had been a soldier they'd have sounded "The Last Post".)

2 Bobby Gould (West Ham United), causing him to be substituted at half-time during the 1974 third round cup-tie against Southampton. (Cracking clue: It made him a leg-end in his own lifetime.)

3 Jack Charlton (Leeds United), *after* the semi-final match against Chelsea in 1967. (Cracking clue: He was hopping mad about it.)

Answers:

1 A goalpost. Cutler ran into it, and the goal collapsed. Once it had been fixed Butler made Wolves collapse, scoring the only goal of the game.

2 His leg. An X-ray showed that Gould had played the last 30 minutes of the half with a fractured leg. And he'd scored a goal before that!

3 His walking stick.  Charlton, Leeds' central defender, hadn't been playing because he was injured and having to use a walking stick. At the end of the match, which Leeds had lost after having a goal disallowed, Charlton was so annoyed he broke his stick in half and had to hop home without it!

PHENOMENAL FA CUP FINALS: 1973 LEEDS UNITED V. SUNDERLAND

Phenomenal Finals are remembered for different things. Some are remembered for their great goals, some for their disputed deciders, others for their injured 'eroes.

The 1973 final was different. It's remembered for one of the most phenomenally flashing and stunningly sensational saves ever seen at Wembley. You could recreate the scene in your playground. Here's how.

- Find 24 players and pick out two squads of twelve each – but don't make it a fair choice.

Leeds United

- Put the best 12 players in one squad. Call them Leeds United. (In 1973, Leeds didn't just have one international player in their squad, they had 11!)

- The other twelve players go into the second squad. They're Sunderland. Everybody thinks they're not in the same league as Leeds – and in one way they're right. Leeds have just finished third in the First Division and are in the final of the European

93

Cup Winners' Cup. Sunderland have spent much of the season struggling in the Second Division!

- Now decide who's going to pretend to be who. Hold trials for the player in the Leeds squad with the hardest shot. Somebody who can knock a hole in the playground wall or remove a teacher's head with a shot from the half-way line is ideal. Call him or her Peter Lorimer. He was Leeds' shooting star, with a thunderbolt shot fast enough to be given a speeding ticket if it had travelled down a motorway.

- Another Leeds squad member, somebody good at diving headers, needs to be chosen to play the part of the Leeds full-back Trevor Cherry.
- The Sunderland squad must do the same, but for a goalkeeper. The best choice is somebody who gives their team-mates kittens with their habit of fumbling the ball and then picking it up again. He or she is going to be Jim Montgomery. They're going to be a hero!

Done all this? Then get ready. It's the 65th minute and Sunderland, to everybody's amazement, are 1-0 ahead after scoring a goal in the first half...

- Have a crowd of you charge into the Sunderland penalty area. Leeds are surging onto the attack.

- A Leeds player swings over the ball from the right wing. In rushes Trevor Cherry from the left wing and meets it with a diving header.

- The ball is sizzling into the opposite corner. Jim Montgomery – dive full-length!

- No, you don't catch the ball. The best you can do is push it to one side ... right into the path of the onrushing Peter Lorimer!
- Peter Lorimer, race in! If you

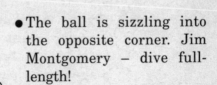

hit it like you usually do you're going to burst the net and send the ball into orbit – but, for some reason you don't. Instead you try to make sure by side-footing the ball into the gaping goal. (Don't tap it, though. A Peter Lorimer side-foot shot is still harder than most players can hit!) The ball whistles towards the net. It must be the Leeds equalizer...

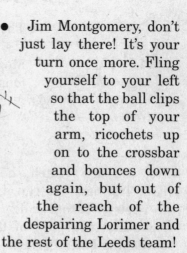

● Jim Montgomery, don't just lay there! It's your turn once more. Fling yourself to your left so that the ball clips the top of your arm, ricochets up on to the crossbar and bounces down again, but out of the reach of the despairing Lorimer and the rest of the Leeds team!

● Sunderland defenders, boot the ball to safety. You've survived!!

That's how it went. Leeds continued to attack, but the save had inspired the Sunderland team. They held on until, thought their frantic captain Bobby Kerr, there couldn't be more than four or five minutes to go. But he couldn't be sure – so he asked the only person who knew, the referee Mr Burns.

Twenty seconds later, Mr Burns blew his whistle. And who said referees were rotten sports?

ROUSING RECORDS... AND ROTTEN RECORDS

See if you can clock up a record score by testing your knowledge with this six-pack of questions about historic happenings in the FA Cup. Every question is to do with a record of some sort.

1 What record did Blackburn Rovers and West Bromwich Albion set in the FA Cup Final of 1886?
a) It was the first final with both teams from outside London.
b) It was the earliest final between teams which are still playing today.
c) It was the first all-Second Division final.

2 What record did Lincoln City and Coventry City set in the third round of the 1963 FA Cup? (Historic hint: It was snow joke at the time!)

3 What semi-final record did Portsmouth and Liverpool set in 1992?
a) It was the first semi-final to be decided by a penalty shoot-out.
b) It was the first semi-final with all the goals coming from penalties.
c) It was the first semi-final in which a goalkeeper scored a penalty.

4 What record was set by James Prinsep of Clapham Rovers in 1879? (Historic hint: It's the oldest and youngest FA Cup record.)

5 What was Manchester United manager Tommy Docherty's record before his team went out to play Liverpool in 1977?

a) He'd never won at Wembley as a player.

b) He'd never won at Wembley as a manager.

c) He'd never won at Wembley as a player or a manager.

6 What record did King George V set at the 1914 Final? (Historic hint: It was the FA Cup's crowning moment.)

Answers:

1b) All the finals before 1886 featured at least one team that no longer play in the competition.

2 It was the most postponed cup-tie ever. In the wicked winter of 1963, Lincoln and Coventry's third round match was postponed 15 times.

Instead of being played on 5 January the game finally took place on 7 March.

THE TEAM WITH THE MOST DETERMINED CAPTAIN ON SNOWY DAYS AWARD...

Gillingham. In 1987 their courageous captain walked six miles through thick snow to join the rest of the team for their third round cup-tie against Wigan – only to find that the game had been called off!

GAME OFF!

THE TEAM WITH THE BEST-NAMED CAPTAIN FOR SNOWY DAYS AWARD...

Gillingham again. Their courageous captain's name was Mark ... Weather!

I'M STUCK WITH THIS NAME, WEATHER I LIKE IT OR NOT!

3a) After a 1-1 draw, then 0-0 in the replay after extra time, Liverpool won on penalties ... leaving Ports-mouth down-in-the-mouth!

4 He was the youngest player ever to appear in an FA Cup Final. Nowadays players take off their long trousers and put on their shorts. In 1879, when footballers played in long trousers, James the Junior almost had to do things the other way round and take off his short trousers. He was only 17 years and 245 days old when he played for Clapham Rovers against Old Etonians.

5c) Docherty had lost as a player with Preston in 1954, and as a manager with Chelsea in 1967 and Manchester United in 1976. He'd also lost at Wembley four times as an international with Scotland. When his team beat Liverpool for his first Wembley win he was so excited he turned cartwheels in London's Hyde Park the next day.

YIPPEEEEE!

6 He was the first reigning monarch to attend the FA Cup Final, where he presented the trophy to the winners.

Rotten records

The FA Cup is littered with records of a different kind. These are really rotten records, though — mainly because most footballers are really rotten singers! Yes, the records we're talking about are the ones lots of Cup Final teams have made for their fans to sing along with.

Can you match the teams with the titles? And, as an extra, pick the one you think got to the highest spot in the Hit Parade?

(A) WEST HAM UNITED (1975)
(B) TOTTENHAM HOTSPUR (1981)
(C) EVERTON (1985)
(D) COVENTRY CITY (1987)
(E) LIVERPOOL (1988)
(F) CRYSTAL PALACE (1990)
(G) ARSENAL (1998)

(1) HERE WE GO
(2) ANFIELD RAP
(3) GLAD ALL OVER
(4) HOT STUFF
(5) GO FOR IT
(6) I'M FOREVER BLOWING BUBBLES
(7) OSSIE'S DREAM

Answers:

A6 The team were a lot more successful than the record of their theme song. West Ham beat Fulham of the Second Division 2-0 in 1975, but the record got no higher than a miserable number 31 in the Hit Parade.

B7 The song was named after their midfield

player at the time (and later their manager), the Argentine international and World Cup winner, Ossie Ardiles. Ossie became an FA Cup winner too, as Spurs beat Manchester City – and the record got to number 5!

THE WORST CUP FINAL "RHYME WITH WEMBLEY" AWARD

"Ossie's Dream", which contained the majestic lines:

♪ "OSSIE'S GOING TO WEMBLEY, ♫ HIS KNEES HAVE GONE ALL TREMBLEY"

C1 "Here We Go" went up to number 14 in the charts ... but Everton went down to a 1-0 defeat against Manchester United.

D5 A far more successful Cup Final "go" than Everton's, but a useless record; Coventry beat Tottenham 3-2 to win the FA Cup for the first time in their history, but their song got no higher than number 61.

E2 After the name of Liverpool's regularly-packed ground, Anfield. The whole crowd must have bought it, too – "Anfield Rap" got to the number 3 spot! It was no consolation for what happened in the FA Cup Final, though. (See "Phenomenal FA Cup Finals: 1988")

I SEE YOU'RE DOING THE ANFIELD WRAP!

F3 A better title would have been "Sad All Over". Palace lost to Manchester United 1-0 in a replay after drawing at Wembley 3-3 and their record only reached number 50.

G4 Just like Arsenal, who won both the League and the FA Cup that year. "Hot Stuff" reached number 9, probably helped by the fact that it was a well-known song and also connected with Arsenal. It was well-known because it had been used in a smash-hit film called *The Full Monty*, about a group of men who become striptease artists! The connection with Arsenal? Part of the men's dance routine has them moving forward in a line with their hands in the air, just like the Arsenal defence asking for an offside decision!

One Wembley song wasn't made into a record (though it might have done better than many that were).

The 1981 FA Cup between Manchester City and Tottenham Hotspur (the 100th Final) was watched by Her Majesty the Queen Mother. As she arrived, both sets of supporters began singing:

"There's only one Queen Mother..."

OF COURSE THERE IS ONLY ONE OF ONE, ONE KNOWS THAT

PHENOMENAL FA CUP FINALS: 1988 LIVERPOOL V. WIMBLEDON

Wimbledon were no strangers to FA Cup shocks. In 1975 their third-round tie against Burnley had seen one of the biggest giant-killing acts in the competition's history. Why was it a shock?

Answer: Because in 1975 Burnley were in the First Division (the highest division in those days) ... and Wimbledon weren't even in the League! They were a Southern League team, only being elected to the then Fourth Division in 1978.

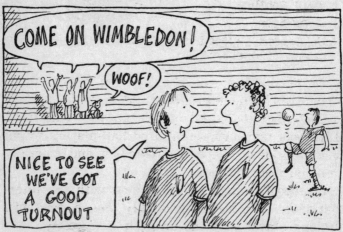

After that, Wimbledon had risen rapidly through the divisions. Or, rather, "charged rapidly". Their tactics won them a lot of games, but didn't win them too many friends. They were simple. Here's how to get the players in your school team playing the Wimbledon Way.

GOALKEEPER:
Whenever you get the ball, immediately kick it as high and as far as you can upfield.

DEFENDERS:
Do exactly the same thing as the goalkeeper (but remember not to pick the ball up!).

FORWARDS:
Chase the ball when it arrives and either score a goal or stop the other team from getting the ball out of their half.

MIDFIELD:
Not needed. Choose to be a defender or an attacker instead.

At least, this was the view of Wimbledon's opponents in the newspapers and on the field. Their tactics would be cruelly shown up, they said, by a Liverpool team whose cultured ball-players would use the wide open spaces of Wembley and generally run rings round them.

Liverpool's squad was crammed with ten internationals. Wimbledon had only one, a Northern Ireland player with the un-Irish name of Lawrie Sanchez. Probably their best known player was an ex-building site labourer named Vinnie Jones. What had brought him to the public's attention? Was it...?

a) A video he'd starred in about dirty play.

b) A newspaper photograph showing him grabbing Paul Gascoigne's dangly bits during a match.

c) Receiving the fastest ever yellow card in FA Cup history – after just three seconds!

Answer: All three, but especially **b).**

So, when the 1988 FA Cup Final began, Liverpool couldn't have been hotter favourites if they'd sprinkled themselves with pepper. But Wimbledon had trained for the match in their own way. How? Was it...?

a) By going to the pub the night before.

b) By giving Dave Beasant, their captain and goalkeeper, penalty-saving practise.

Answer: **a)** and **b)!**

After a session during which Wimbledon players Alan Cork and Denis Wise hit penalties at Beasant, placing them in exactly the same way as Liverpool's penalty-taker John Aldridge, their manager, Bobby Gould, sent them all off to a pub to relax. Cork played a leading part in this session as well. He woke up with such a pounding headache he had to wear dark glasses on the coach to Wembley because he found the sun too bright!

JUST POINT ME IN THE RIGHT DIRECTION!

THE MOST POPULAR BALD-HEADED WIMBLEDON PLAYER AWARD...

Alan Cork, who played for Wimbledon throughout their rise up the League. The Wimbledon fans would greet him with the cry, "He's got no hair, but we don't care!"

Relaxed or not, it was the penalty-taking session that won Wimbledon the Cup. Lawrie Sanchez had given them a surprise lead in the first half, but Liverpool were fighting back and in the sixty-first minute they were awarded a penalty. Up stepped Liverpool's Aldridge. It was his 12th penalty of the season. How many of the previous 11 had he missed?

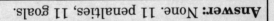

Answer: None. 11 penalties, 11 goals.

But not this time. As he placed his shot in his usual spot, the Wimbledon training session paid off. Beasant dived to his left and saved the kick – the first ever penalty save in a Wembley Final.

Thirty minutes later, Beasant's gloves were being wrapped round something else. The FA Cup. Wimbledon had hung on to win 1-0.

THE PRETTIEST FOOTBALLER'S LEG AWARD...

Vinnie Jones. To celebrate Wimbledon's victory, he had a picture of the FA Cup and the words, "FA Cup Winners, 1988" tattooed on his leg.

After Wimbledon's victory, a lot of newspaper forecasters and football experts had to eat their words. And it's certainly not the only time *that's* happened...

• In 1976 the four semi-finalists were Manchester United and Derby County of the First Division, Southampton of the Second and Crystal Palace of the Third. When Manchester United and Derby were drawn against each other United manager Tommy Docherty said:

THIS IS THE FIRST TIME THE FA CUP FINAL WILL BE PLAYED AT HILLSBOROUGH. THE OTHER SEMI-FINAL IS A BIT OF A JOKE REALLY.

Then, when Southampton and United won through to the Final, United's winger (or should that be whinger?), Gordon Hill, said:

WHO ARE SOUTHAMPTON?

He soon found out. Southampton won 1-0!

• Steve Ogrizovic, Coventry City's goalkeeper and captain, was a bit more polite when Coventry came up against non-league Sutton United in the third round in 1989.

WE SHOULD BEAT SUTTON, BUT IT WON'T BE A LANDSLIDE, JUST A THOROUGHLY PROFESSIONAL PERFORMANCE

He should have said a thoroughly phenomenally pathetic performance: Coventry lost 2-1!

- Dave Bassett, manager of Wimbledon, Sheffield United and others, was once very enthusiastic about his team's chances – in an unenthusiastic sort of way:

I HONESTLY BELIEVE WE CAN GO ALL THE WAY TO WEMBLEY...UNLESS SOMEBODY KNOCKS US OUT!

PHENOMENAL FA CUP FINAL DAY

It's the big day! Your team have won their way through round after round and now you're there – at Wembley, on Cup Final day.

What's going to happen? Will it be your year?

Maybe your team will be like Tottenham Hotspur. All they had to do during the 20th century was look at the calendar. If the year ended in a "1" then they knew everything was going to be all right. After first lifting the FA Cup in 1901 they went on to win it in 1921, 1961, 1981 and 1991 (as well as in 1962, 1967 and 1982).

It's the biggest day of your footballing career. Ever since you first began diving on your bed as you imagined yourself making super saves or scoring with heroic headers you've been dreaming of this day. But will it turn out to be a dream ... or a nightmare?

Here's your step-by-step checklist for this phenomenal Final day – together with the odd story about where it all went wrong for some players and turned into a foul Final day!

Wembley way

After a leisurely morning and a leisurely lunch, you jump on the team coach and head for the ground in good time ... almost like Blackburn Olympic did in 1886. They had a leisurely morning, watching the Oxford v. Cambridge Boat Race on the Thames, then a leisurely lunch. But they'd been a bit too leisurely and ended up having to race to the ground at Kennington Oval before they missed the kick-off!

Where's your tickets, then?

You hop off the coach, get a salute from the Wembley security men, and go straight into the ground ... except that that's not quite what happened to Barnsley when they turned up at the Crystal Palace for their final against Newcastle United in 1910. Somebody had forgotten to bring their

special tickets – and the
commissionaire on the door
wouldn't let them in! He only
relented when a Football
League official told him that
he was locking out the
Barnsley team and if he didn't
let them in quick there'd be
no Final. Not fancying the
thought of 77,747 fans
chasing him down the road,

the commissionaire backed down and the game
went ahead, ending in a 1-1 draw. (Maybe the
commissionaire should have gone up to the replay at
Goodison Park and stopped Newcastle getting in –
they beat Barnsley 2-0 to lift the trophy.)

The dodgy dressing room

In you go, to your Wembley dressing room. But is it
the lucky one, or the unlucky one?

The two dressing rooms at Wembley are known as
the North and South dressing rooms. (They were
until 2000, anyway. Then Wembley was knocked
down for rebuilding and they both went west!)
Superstitious footballers believed that the South

dressing room was luckier than the North. How did the superstition arise?

a) Because England always used South.

b) Because three times more Cup-winners have used South than used North.

c) Because the first four winning finalists after World War Two all used South.

116

NO, YOU CAN'T CHANGE YOUR NAME FROM ABSHOT ALBION TO ZUZU ZULUS!

SPOIL SPORT

All change!

It's time to get your kit on and talk about the game to come. Maybe even make a prophecy, like Tottenham Hotspur's striker Jimmy Greaves did in 1962. He predicted he'd score against Spurs' opponents Burnley after only four minutes – but he was wrong. He scored after only three minutes and Spurs went on to win the match 3-1.

Have a sing-song

OOOH, THEY'RE SINGING MY FAVOURITE SONG!

Maybe you won't be singing in the dressing room, but outside the fans will be.

In 1927 the Wembley crowd began the tradition of "community singing", in which everybody joined in together to sing popular tunes of the time. This lasted for a long while, until fans decided they knew better and ruder songs and that if they

117

bawled them loudly enough they could drown out the official songs.

But one song has lasted since its first appearance in 1927, and is still part of the pre-match tradition. It's a hymn called "Abide With Me". Who chose it?

a) King George V and Queen Mary, guests of honour in 1927.

b) The 1927 Cup Final referee, Mr W. F. Bunnell.

c) Cardiff City's 1927 winning captain, Fred Keenor.

Answer: The King and Queen. Written by a Devon vicar shortly before he died in 1847, it was their favourite hymn.

> Abide with me, fast falls the eventide.
> The darkness deepens, Lord with me abide.
> When other helpers fail and comforts flee,
> Help of the helpless, O abide with me.

It's a well-liked hymn in Manchester, too!

- Bert Trautmann, Manchester City's German-born goalkeeper in 1956 (he who ended with a broken neck), said...

I THINK IT IS A WONDERFUL THING, AND ONE FOR WHICH BRITISH SPORTS-LOVERS... ARE TO BE RESPECTED

- As for Pat Crerand, Manchester United's star midfield player in 1963, he liked the hymn so much he wanted to join in himself. As the team were getting ready to leave the dressing room,

Crerand couldn't be found. He was out in the player's tunnel, singing along with the crowd! They wouldn't have spotted him as a player, though. He hadn't put his gear on. He was only wearing his undies!

The long walk

It's the big moment for the managers of the two finalists. They get to lead their teams out on to the pitch.

In 1991, though, Nottingham Forest manager Brian Clough and Tottenham Hotspur manager Terry Venables did things a little differently. As well as leading their teams, they led each other as well. To show what a friendly final it was going to be, they walked all the way into the centre of the pitch holding hands!

May I present...

The teams are presented to the Guest of Honour – who should always follow a bit of advice His or Her

Majesty or Royal Highness or whoever has been given by the FA. What is it they're always told *not* to do?

a) Wear something the same colour as one of the teams.

b) Say, "I hope you smash the other lot!"

c) Pick up a football and try to do a bit of juggling.

Answer: a) Guests of Honour are supposed to show they're neutral (even though they may think **b)** and reckon they could do **c)** better than half the players on the pitch).

Kick-off!

The match begins. It's a special occasion, but it's still a match you want to win – as Portsmouth's tough-nut captain, Jimmy Guthrie, quickly made clear in the 1939 Final against Wolverhampton Wanderers.

Before the Portsmouth fans' singing of "Who's Afraid of the Big, Bad Wolf?" had hardly died down, Guthrie had roared in with a crunching tackle on the Wolves left-winger Teddy Maguire and sent him flying. Sportsman Guthrie helped pick him up, of course … only to whisper in his ear,

NEXT TIME YOU FINISH IN THE QUEEN'S LAP!

Score the winning goal!

But try not to get substituted, like Roger Osborne of Ipswich Town against Arsenal in 1978.

With just 13 minutes left to play, Osborne whacked the ball into the Arsenal net to put his team 1-0 ahead. Within moments he was at the bottom of a jubilant pyramid of blue-shirted Ipswich players all celebrating the goal. Not so much Osborne as Os-gorne! When he finally got up, rocky Roger couldn't even raise enough energy to get back to the centre-circle for the kick-off. He had to be substituted at once!

"The exhaustion and all the excitement were just too much for me," he said afterwards.

HOOO-RAY!

Winners! Collect your losers' medals!

At the start of the game the FA Cup would have been on show, decked out with ribbons in the colours of both teams. Now there'll just be your team's ribbons. You've won the Cup! It's time to climb the famous steps up to the Royal Box to collect your winner's medal...

...unless you'd been playing in the 1992 FA Cup Final. That year, the procedure got changed around. Until then the winning team had gone up first to collect the cup and their medals. This had meant nobody took a lot of notice of the losers when their turn came, because all eyes were on the new Cup-winners.

So in 1992 it was decided that the losers, Sunderland, would go up first and the winners, Liverpool, would go up second. That bit went smoothly. Where it went wrong was that the order in which the medals were given out by the Duke & Duchess of Kent *didn't* change – the sad Sunderland players found themselves with winners' medals, and leaping Liverpool became losing Liverpool! They had to sort it all out in the dressing rooms later.

Most Cup-winners get more than a medal, though. Their clubs usually pay them a nice fat bonus. Except that, after pulling off their surprise win against Wolverhampton Wanderers in 1939, the Portsmouth players thought the £50 they were given was more of a bony bonus than a fat one – especially when they found out that another group of people at Wembley had earned more. Who were they?

a) The referee and linesmen.

b) The brass bands who'd entertained the crowd at half-time.

c) The Wembley groundsmen.

THEY THINK IT'S ALL OVER

You're the Cup-winners. There's only one thing left to do now – celebrate!

Triumphant tours and home hoorays

Nowadays teams tour the town on the top decks of coaches and buses far out of the reach of the fans. All a far cry from 1883. When Blackburn Olympic arrived home with the FA Cup they jumped on to a horse-drawn wagon for a quick trip round the streets. Their fans were looking down on them!

Then, without fail, the trophy will be paraded in front of the fans at the next home match and given all the sumptuous glory it deserves. Unless the fans are Arsenal's in 1930. After they'd beaten Huddersfield 2-0, the Cup was trundled round Highbury before a league match two days later – on a makeshift trolley made out of a wooden box on top of a baby's pram! (Arsenal fans will probably say they were showing how easy it had been for them to win the Cup … child's play, in fact!)

Say "Cup-winner!"

What then? Does the trophy stay locked in the club's trophy cabinet all year? Not if you're Chelsea it doesn't. After winning the FA Cup in 1997, they allowed fans to be photographed holding it at £15 a time. How many takers did they get?

a) 10 a month.

b) 100 a month.

c) 1,000 a month.

Answer: c) That's £15,000 a month for 12 months – £180,000. Enough to buy well over a dozen FA Cups!

So, who will win the FA Cup this year? Which fancied team will fall victim to a bunch of giant-killers? Will the famous trophy be carried off by a team of household names or a team whose names are only known in their own houses?

One thing's for sure. Just like every year, the competition will feature games that are foul, games that are frantic and games that are phenomenal. And any player who does get a winner's medal will be phenomenally proud.

THE PROUDEST FA CUP WINNING CAR-DRIVING PLAYER AWARD...

Jim Standen, goalkeeper in West Ham's 1964 Cup-winning team. On moving to California, where you're allowed to pick your own car number plates, he chose:

FA CUP 64

But that's only to be expected. Because winning the FA Cup is never foul, it may sometimes be frantic ... but it's always phenomenal!